Edited by Joe McD(

GW00761219

Voices in the Wilderness?

YOUNG PEOPLE
AND THE CHURCH

the columba press

the columba press
8 Lower Kilmacud Road, Blackrock, Co Dublin, Ireland

First edition 1987
Cover by Bill Bolger
Calligraphy by Angela Hickey
Photographs by Jackie Curtis
Typesetting by Typeform, Dublin
Printed in Ireland by Criterion Press, Dublin

ISBN 0 948183 39 X

Contents

The Contributors:

Kieran Byrne is 26 years old. He is full-time involved in Retreat work in Tabor House. He has studied social science and has recently completed the course in Catechetics in Mount Oliver.

Tony Flynn is 22 year old. He is from Cork, and working in a Pharmaceutical Company. Tony has been involved in YCW.

Paula Goggin is 23 years old. She is presently studying in Mater Dei Institute. Paula is from Tullow, Co. Carlow.

Damien Killen is 24 year old. He is married to Niamh. He graduated for Trinity College as a social worker and is at present working full-time with the Faith Development Team in the Catholic Youth Council.

Dearbhla McArdle is 24 years old. She is from Carlow and is working there as a carpenter at present. She studied design in Carlow RTC.

Marie Moore is 21 years old. She is from Cork and at present is working as a receptionist. She is involved with a folk group and Muintearas Íosa.

Bishop Donal Murray is titular Bishop of Glendalough and an Auxiliary Bishop of Dublin.

Mick Peelo is 27 years old. He is a full-time student of theology. He is married and living in Dublin. Mick has been involved with Resource Magazine for some time.

Toni Walsh is 24 years old. She is working in primary school education. She is married and living in Dublin. Toni has been involved with the 'Laudate' tape and many other related activities.

Introduction

In November 1985, the Irish Bishops issued a Pastoral Letter addressed to 'all concerned with the pastoral care of young people'. It was entitled 'The Young Church'. Central to this letter was the invitation from the Bishops – 'We want to listen to you . . . your hungers and your hurts, your attitudes in many areas, including your experience of the Church in Ireland now'. (*The Young Church*, page 5).

In November 1987, a synod of Bishops from all over the world will be held in Rome, to discuss the laity and their role in the Church.

During 1986 a limited form of consultation of lay people took place, in preparation for the Synod. The results were communicated to the Bishops for their consideration.

As of yet no one knows what the Irish Bishops are going to say on behalf of the lay members of the Church – or what will be contained in the report to be submitted to Rome in preparation for the Synod.

In the process of consultation, it seems that very few young people were involved in expressing their views – the 'voice' of young people was at best very mute.

This book provides a 'voice' for some young people who wish to speak. It makes no claim to be a representative voice. It is written in response to the Bishops' declaration 'we want to listen to you . . .'.

It is also written in the hope that it might be used by different groups, e.g. senior classes in schools, and others involved in discussing Church and relevant issues today.

The young people who wrote reflections for the book took as their starting point the areas of interest that emerged during the weekend in Teach Bríde. It is likely that the way in which these areas are dealt with by one group of young people would evoke a response from many others. With this in mind, questions have been included at the end of each reflection which we hope will stimulate discussion and raise further questions.

Bishop Donal Murray read the reflections and agreed to contribute a response, which is included here as the final chapter.

The book results from a lot of work by a lot of people and we would like particularly to acknowledge the following:

The Contributors
Fintan Farrell
Brid Maguire
Jackie Curtis
Angela Hickey
and the forty-seven voices,
including the eight team-members
who facilitated the weekend.

47 Voices

A report on the weekend for young people, held at Teach Bríde, Tullow, Co. Carlow, in Autumn 1986.

A group of forty-seven young people came together for a weekend recently to share their experiences, their hopes, their fears, their sadnesses, their joys about Church and about life. They were a very varied group – the ages ranged from 17 to 30. Some were very involved in Church, some had no involvement. They came from rural and urban backgrounds. Some were students, others workers, still others unemployed. A small few were educationally and socially disadvantaged. The large number of young people who are alienated and distanced from the Church were represented in only a very limited way. Between all of these people there was a great variety of experiences, backgrounds and expectations. However, it was clear from the outset that this group in no way was representative of young people generally. This report of what was said during the weekend cannot therefore claim to be *the voice* of young people in Ireland, but of one group of varied and concerned young people. Nor is it an agreed statement by the group. Opposing opinions were sometimes expressed and the process did not seek to find a consensus.

The process allowed the group themselves to decide the agenda for the weekend. This was done by spending some time in groups discussing questions like:

What are you happy/unhappy about in your experience of Church?
In what areas of Church life are you interested?
What are your concerns?

The following points emerged from this discussion: The Church is dominated by the clerical group – Pope, bishops, priests. There is no sense in which power is shared. People have no say in decision making. In structure, practice and reality there is no sense of equality among the members. Power is maintained by those at the top of the pyramid – many at the bottom (lay people) experience oppression. 'Priests won't let go of power and control'. Titles, e.g. father, sister, are seen by some as creating barriers. The contradiction between the preaching and the practice of those who preach is a serious issue.

'I believe in God and Jesus, but not in the Church'.

'The Church has very little credibility among young people'.

The Church is seen as something forced on people – people are not free to choose. It was obvious during the weekend that within the group there were several different understandings of 'Church'. Some see the Church as a building, or as the priests only. Some see it as a people. The Church is not really about Christianity – rather about Catholic rules. There is a Church for the rich and powerful and one for the poor and voiceless. Class distinction exists in the Church.

'Where is Christ in the Church – all I see are rules'.

The Church is not very relevant to the life of many people today. It should be about everyday things. Some feel little or no need for the Church.

'We don't need religion to go out on the street and help people'.

Involvement was a key issue for many of those present. Some felt no sense of belonging until they actually became part of a small group or movement, e.g. Muintearas, Young Christian Workers (YCW), Discovery Programme, Folk Group, etc. Some feel that lay involvement in Mass is a token gesture. The language used is mostly irrelevant and often alienating. Some find the sexist language of our liturgies and prayers highly offensive. The lack of feminine involvement at all levels of Church life is a source of anger and frustration to many people.

Worship seems really relevant only when celebrated in small groups. It was generally acknowledged that there is a lack of knowledge and understanding of Church teachings and traditions.

'Language at Mass is a big problem – we just don't understand'.

There is a great deal of confusion about the Church and about its teachings, which is sometimes accompanied by deep anger and hurt.

'Many young people want to be involved in the Church, but you have to wiggle your way in – accepting the values and rules'.

'Try and be Church in your own parish and you will see what it is really like'.

From the foregoing discussion, seven general areas emerged for further reflection and suggestions:

1. Liturgy/Worship/Prayer
2. Structures/Organisation/Power
3. Alienation/Poverty/Social Justice
4. God/Jesus/Love/Faith/Hope
5. Women
6. Community/Belonging/Invitation/Joy/Hope
7. Personal Development/Education

The process allowed for each person to choose which ever area he/she wished to work with over the weekend. Each of the seven groups first discussed their experience, and presented this in drama or role play for the whole group. An opportunity was then given to the total group, to discuss and comment on each of the presentations, using questions like:

Was the presentation real and true to life?
What were the main problems?
What were the causes of these?
What would be needed to bring about changes?

The following is an attempt to summarise the comments on each of these seven areas. Some overlapping was very evident, because of the inter-connectedness between the various areas.

1. Liturgy/Worship/Prayer

By and large the experience of liturgy is monotonous, boring and routine. 'It's a *one man* show mostly' – the priest who takes part as if in a monologue while the people are passive.

Some people feel totally alienated in the normal Sunday Mass situation. Others are happy about it, particularly through involvement with a folk group or choir.

'We have lost the ability to celebrate'. 'We don't know who we are celebrating with'. The changes already introduced 'are just the same way of doing things except by different people'.

For change to happen, liturgies will have to reflect much more the lived experience of those involved. In situations where this has happened, the liturgies are always enriching.

'There is a need for more imagination and creativity'. 'It

would also be helpful if people were educated regarding liturgy'.

2. *Structures/Organisation/Power*

There are several varied perceptions of the Church among young people. 'Top-down authority is exercised in the Church'. Decisions are made by very few. Priests often abuse their authority. Power and its control is maintained at the top of the pyramid.

'There is no room for questioning within the Church'. Communication within the Church is 'very bad'. 'There is no encouragement and no invitation given to those who feel outside'.

Many people possess a very poor understanding of the Church. People have no say in the appointment of leaders. 'Some young people are very unsure of whether or not they belong'. Some feel that the traditional Church is reaching out and trying to make itself relevant.

People's talents are not used in parishes generally. 'There is a lot of anger among a lot of people about the Church'.

Change could happen, if those in control and authority, e.g. bishops, become more open-minded and if they were really genuine in their invitation to listen. This would lead to better communication. 'The language needs to be simple'. Real consultation must take place and not the tokenism of recent times. Decision-making needs to be shared.

'Education and formation of the laity is necessary and essential for change'.

If an acknowledgement was made that 'the way things are is not the only way things can be', then change might be possible.

3. Alienation/Poverty/Social Justice

Justice means taking sides – being involved. A serious question was asked about how an organisation can preach and demand justice, when it is unjust within itself. The Church often seems to take the side of the oppressor. 'The Church has much material resources and wealth, and with this comes power'. Lay people have no say in the spending of their own money in the Church.

Because of language and presentation, Church documents and statements are inaccessible to the majority of people and so have no relevance. The Third World suffers from massive injustice but what of the home front? What about unemployment, and the Church's concern for justice? We are part of an 'individualistic' non-political, charity-orientated Church'. Much of the oppression in people's lives is because of the economic system which is maintained in this country, and the Church helps maintain it – it must be changed. 'The Church is not identifying with the poor – as Jesus Christ did'. The power of the people to bring about change, e.g. Philippines, is a resource that has been untapped. The established Church needs to support those who fight for justice. True justice must be based on compassion and love.

We must acknowledge that we live in a capitalist society – change will come only through action. Many good things are happening, e.g. the recent CMRS/NCPI publication entitled 'Shaping Our Future (Work, Jobs and Unemployment: A Christian Response)', Traidcraft, programmes such as 'Partners in Mission' and 'Training for Transformation', etc. Are we aware of them, do we avail of them?

'How do we use our vote? We should vote for people who hold Christian values'. Non-church groups who are working for justice, e.g. Unemployment Action groups should be actively supported. 'The credibility of the Church is at stake in this area!' 'People at the top must give us example'.

4. God/Faith/Jesus/Love/Hope

The idea that whatever happens 'is God's will' is still very prevalent. Some feel that the Church has been responsible for much of this emphasis; it helps keep control, keeps down reactionary people and leads to apathy.

Faith is just a habit for many people, because they were born into it and reared in it; it has never been personalised. For many, faith and God has to do with individualistic salvation, and not with community. God seems to be a word used to describe all the things we don't understand. God reveals him/herself through justice an peace. 'Faith and justice are linked'. The Creed was felt to be irrelevant to most people. It's language is archaic – it needs rewriting. 'It is sexist . . . "for us men" '. There are several different images for God and Church. No one of them is complete in itself. To see only one is to distort the truth. 'Private and liturgical prayer are both very important'.

For change to happen it is essential to empower all people. 'Let us find our own way to faith – let it not be pushed on us'. There are many signs of hope, e.g. Focus Point in Dublin.

5. Women

We are conditioned into thinking in terms of *man* made in the image of God. Church language reflects this, as does involvement in various special ministries. Decision-making in the Church is a male preserve. Many women are very passive about these issues. Women's lack of involvement in the Church is but a reflection of the same in society at large. On the whole, culture is male-dominated.

Enormous variation in levels of awareness about this issue exist across the board. Some see no problem about the position of women in the Church. 'Many gifted, tired, and angry women have walked away from the Church and continue to do so'.

Change must come about in the language of the Church. However, 'change of language without change of attitude, will achieve very little'. People need to be angered enough by the present situation to be motivated into acting to effect change. We need to hear about the feminine side of God. It is important to note that the Bible was written in a particular age, culture and context.

This is not a 'women's issue' but an issue of justice. 'It's time to stop apologising for the anger and passion that some people feel about this subject'.

By this will all people know that you are my disciples if you have love for one another

6. Community/Belonging/Invitation/Joy/Hope

The size of parishes makes it difficult to build community. To build community requires effort and that often leads to pain. Some acknowledged a lack of interest on behalf of many young people in becoming involved in the local parish or community. Those with power, especially priests, don't trust people enough to share thier power.

Community means making time for people. Personal invitation is the most effective way of getting people involved. Those who get involved risk getting laughed at. Smaller units as parishes are necessary if a sense of community is going to be developed.

7. Personal Development/Education

Religious education is very inadequate. It was generally held that our education system is expensive and gives advantages to the privileged. It is too competitive. Little or no value is attached to learning from experience.

When young people leave school 'religion ends for most'. The onus is on the individuals to develop their faith – but most lack the ability to be responsible for it. Peer pressure is a big problem. The education system maintains the hierarchial structure within which it exists.

'If I was to apply my awareness to the system I am within, I would have to leave it'.

Change can only happen when people become aware of the problems. Laity and clergy need education. Language needs to be changed. Religious education should be the responsibility of the whole community.

'Provide after school education, with programmes for smaller groups'.

'The first step to change is awareness'.

Evaluation of the weekend

Some felt that the task was too enormous to achieve anything of value in so short a period. The very diversity of the group was a difficulty. Some found the whole experience very worthwhile, as it led them to a greater awareness of some of the issues involved. Others felt a good deal of frustration. A few felt they did not fit in.

The better informed were the most articulate and thus they tended to dominate. Others felt their contributions were not heard.

'If less had been said, more would have been remembered'.

It was stated that the experience of the weekend, the diversity of the participants, the domination of some, the voicelessness of others, the stuggle to understand, the search for truth, the friendship experienced, the liturgical celebrations, all were a microcosm of the Church as we experience it.

Listening –
but afraid of hearing

by Marie Moore

I went to Teach Bríde hopeful of spending a pleasant weekend discussing God and his love for us, and the way we live. It turned out to be an eye-opening experience and an education for me. No sooner had the first session begun than I realised I was in for a shock. My cosy picture of Church seemed to be non-existent for many people present. It saddened me to see that they found no joy in 'Church', that the word 'church' meant only anger and bitterness to them.

My first reaction was to become defensive. It seemed to me that when criticising the Church they were criticising God and his love. But what I had to come to terms with was that they were not attacking God when attacking the Church because they did not see God in it. They saw people in authority misrepresenting the Christian ideal by abusing their authority, by turning a blind eye to the faults in the structure of the Church, and by neglecting the needs of the oppressed and the under-priveleged, etc. Many of these were disillusioned and angry.

The weekend showed me the difference in people and how important it is to have such a variety in the Church. For example, if everyone just saw God only in Mass and Church celebrations, rather than in the old, the children, the needy and the suffering – what kind of world would it be?

At times I felt guilty because I did not have to struggle for my religion. But having reflected on it, I realised I had a struggle that was equally difficult as the struggle against the Church's structure. Since I had admitted to the presence of God and claimed to love him, I had an obligation to prove it! Was I doing that? If I admit the presence of God it has to be made visible to others in my life style, in my giving of myself, my time, my love and my understanding. This was my struggle. They say, 'the closer you get to God, the more he asks; and the more he asks the tougher it gets, but the greater the reward'!

For me, God must be seen in other people and in nature, but first and foremost he is a person to be loved and accepted as a friend, who is always there and who loves me.

Someone I know could not understand how I managed to speak of God in such familiar terms. But I felt I could not speak of him in any other way because to me he is as real as anyone I know, and the most valued friend I have. And in my view, a friend is not someone who is distant, cold, emotionless and unreachable, but instead is warm, approachable and very much part of my life. So I thought it right to speak of God in a familiar and natural way. I remember feeling very sad that the person who challeng-ed me about it thought of God as someone distant and to whom one spoke in a reserved manner. I hoped someday she would see him in a more personal way and allow him into the everyday things in her life, and not just be a vague divine image to her when she prayed.

I have found myself echoing that hope over and over again for others when I hear them saying that they do not get anything out of Mass. I think Mass would be mean-ingless and boring to me too if I did not look on it as an opportunity of spending some time with the friend I love and telling him of my needs and where I am at, at that time, and what is troubling me or making me happy, etc.

I have found that being involved in a folk group has helped me to understand the different parts of the Mass better, and attending small group Masses at Muintearas Íosa gatherings has really brought home the idea of the Last Supper, the community sharing, and the value of active participation by everyone in the Mass. But at the same time, I feel that sometimes I get too caught up in all the activity and miss out on the full meaning of what is taking place. Therefore, I value too being able to sit in the body of a big parish church and observe what is happeining and be aware of the mystery which is taking place. But being actually involved is essential for many people, and small group Masses provide excellent opportunities for joyful celebrations.

The Liturgy reflects the faith hope and love of the Community

A small group Mass gives an ideal picture of what Church should be. It is a community of a variety of people, all celebrating the same mystery – sharing the one meal, working together and praising God. My hope and vision would be that the worldwide Church could become a bigger version of this joyful group Mass – where those in authority would work side by side with others in the Church, and where everyone would give strength to each other based on the common belief in the love and mercy of God. Much change is needed to make this vision real and I feel it can be done, but we cannot do it by ourselves. We must find our strength in God and our hope in the love we have for each other.

By the end of the 'Church weekend', all seemed to agree on one thing at least – the structure of the Church needed changing and those in authority need to listen to what everyone had to say. But in our struggle we must not lose sight of God and love.

I am really grateful to the 'Church weekend' for opening my eyes to so many different views and for helping me to understand what is going on in the hearts and heads of other people of my own age. I am one of those in the young Church and yet I was so unaware of much of what was going on for others in the young Church until I met and listened to what they had to say. So what hope have the Bishops and those in authority of providing for our needs if they do not listen to us too?

Questions
1. What makes you happy/unhappy about your experience of the Church, especially in your local parish?
2. What can you do to make your parish more relevant to young people?
3. Dialogue is necessary. Can you bring people together to discuss matters of religious interest – young people, adults, religious, etc?

Towards a Church fully alive

by Damien Killen

Once upon a time, there was a land where the people attended Church regularly. On one Sunday in every year their leader read the gospel reading of 'the harvest is plentiful, and the labourers are few' (Lk 10:2). The people prayed to God, to ask him to select one of them to be a future leader. Every other year one young man came forward and he was sent away to be trained in how to listen to God and on how to tell the people what God really wanted from them.

The people were a very contented lot. If they ever wanted to know about God, or talk to him, or find out what he was saying they went to their leader who gave them all the answers. In this land everything was black and white.

As time went on fewer and fewer young men were coming forward. Their leader encouraged them to pray harder. Each year they prayed harder. However, the years went by and eventually no one came forward. The worried leader thought, prayed, and wondered what he could do, until one year he decided that on the special Sunday when everyone prayed for new leaders to come forward, he would change the reading. He chose 'the Kingdom of God is within you' (Lk 17:21). The people who had grown accustomed to the same reading were surprised. 'What does this mean'? they thought.

Over the following week many of the people went to their leader to ask him what 'God was really saying'. He told them to ask God themselves what God was saying to them and to ask him what he wanted them to do.

Everyone seemed to be confused. There were no more right answers. But in the land there appeared to be shades of grey among the black and white.

As time passed more and more people started asking questions about what it could mean. Some began reading other parts of the Gospel.

The following year the leader read the Parable of the Talents (Lk 19:12-27).

More questions as to what should be done! Slowly but surely a recognition that God was alive in each person and that each one had talents to be used to build God's Kingdom on earth, dawned on the people.

That year many people came forward not wanting to be the leader, but to play a part in bringing God's message, in word and deed, to their brothers and sisters.

The people were no longer contented or confused but rather excited and alive. In this land colours abounded.

Friday night . . . Teach Bríde . . . 'Church' Weekend . . .

Those present were asked to describe their experiences and images of 'Church'. Inevitably and not surprisingly the response described a Church 'which is heavily dominated by the clergy . . . a place where there was no sharing of power . . . one which contradicted itself with its teaching and the practice of those who teach . . . unfair to women . . . hierarchical . . . traditional'. All this is usually labelled by theologians, church*men* and 'those who know', and the 'institutional' Church. No matter what name is put on it, this is how the majority of young Irish people see the 'Church'.

Gradually the question arose as to whether the Church

was a building or people, and whether if it meant people, how much a part of it were we? Many of those present said they never felt a part of the Church until they became involved in something, usually a small group, e.g. Young Christian Workers (YCW), Discovery, Muintearas, etc., or until they began a personal relationship with God, e.g. while on retreat.

However, when the theme of community was explored in more detail the following day by some of the group, these last experiences of Church were often over-looked. Ultimately, for most, community equalled parish, and as a result, more of the critical feelings outlined above, surfaced.

The size of the parish was said to contribute to the difficulty encountered in trying to build community. Power structures within parishes were seen to limit the involvement of people. Because of such situations it was felt that there is a lack of interest by the young people themselves in becoming involved in their parish.

Why is it that when asked to illustrate their image of Church and of community, young people (who are involved) depict the 'institutional' image rather than one which is more in keeping with their own experience?

Is it because the message portrayed by the leaders of the Church is different to their positive experience? – and yet despite being untrue, can overwhelm their own impressions? Or is it that they have never been taught to recognise Christ and his values in their own midst?

Changes

The group that looked at this theme suggested that 'we need to work in smaller units than the traditional parish unit, if we hope to be able to build a sense of community'.

The ways to achieve this are already present in the Irish Church. The positive experiences of some, needs to be made a reality for all. A brief survey of 'what has worked' for young people over the past decade will immediately highlight the importance of small groups. Here young people can experience belonging, a sense of being important, a sense of being valued for who they are. Here everybody's opinion counts.

For the small group process to be relevant to today and to be true to the Gospel and the Church's tradition, it needs to include four elements (neatly summarised in Acts 2:42-47):

1. Fellowship and friendship among a group of people.
2. Breaking bread together – faith sharing, celebrating and prayer.
3. Looking at the scriptures.
4. Outreach to and service to others.

Each of these elements, respectively, meets different needs that we have:

1. To love and be loved.
2. To celebrate together, share our ideas and be understood.
3. Meaning and purpose.
4. To act justly and serve others.

These elements are not new and as mentioned already are present in some of today's groups. For example, programmes such as 'Discovery', 'Choice', etc, enable young people to come together in a friendly atmosphere to discuss issues that are relevant to their lives, with a chance to celebrate this in Eucharist.

The Young Christian Workers (YCW) encourages groups to look at the gospels and their meaning for today, through their 'enquiries'. Their method of 'see-judge-act' is important in leading the group to do something with their 'new understanding'. Prayer groups and St Vincent de Paul conferences are good examples of where the third and fourth elements are being met repectively. This outreach and study of scripture should ensure that the groups do not become too insular or a 'holy huddle'. There are many more groups such as Muintearas Íosa, Student Christian Movement (SCM), Youth-in-Action, Basic Christian Communities (some in Dublin), People's Mass (Ballymun), Focolare . . ., the list is endless. Not all groups encompass all four elements but it is an ideal towards which many are or should be striving. The signs of hope are before our eyes.

Establishing groups with these elements is in essence building 'community', by building small living cells. When appropriate these small groups, living cells, can be brought together for larger community gatherings.

How can young (and not so young!) people be encouraged to build these living cells? Initially, they need to be invited to take part. Then the listening process must begin in order that trust can be established. A sense of belonging will only emerge once someone feels that they are important to the group (and visa versa), and are given some responsibility. It is this last area of responsibility that is vital to the survival and ultimately to the growth of these cells. A Church will never be alive if everyone is excluded from playing his/her part. Vatican II recognised that youth 'must be the prime apostles to youth' (Decree on Laity, para. 9).

What this means — the challenge
This has implications for every one of us, who consider him/herself a part of the Church.

The Church needs to be perceived differently by young

Co-Creators of this world with God

people in order that its mission, i.e. remembering Jesus in word and deed, can be achieved. The image of Church as only a building, or as a bureaucratic organisation with an hierarchical model of power, needs to be displaced by the image of groups of people where everyone has a part to play in its mission. This can only be achieved by those in power being prepared to share that power and by them encouraging others to become involved; and by everyone recognising that as baptised Christians they are members of the Church and thus have a role to undertake.

For living cells to be effective and contribute to building a living Church the small group concept will have to be believed in. At one simple level this will mean a change away from 'getting Mass' in a Church that more resembles an 'aircraft hanger' than a place of worship, towards more intimate gatherings, where everyone can contribute as they please.

In addition opportunities need to be created within communities (and within parishes) where young people come together to talk about issues that are important to them, and where they can celebrate this together in prayer and liturgy – in a liturgy that is real and true to their lives rather than cold and removed from them.

As a sense of belonging is established, hopefully the

uniqueness and giftedness of each individual will be both recognised and valued. As a result the role that each person can play within the community will become more apparent, be it visiting old folks, running a baby-sitting-service, helping with the communion programme in the parish, establishing a prayer group, co-ordinating activities in the youth clubs, etc. 'There are as many ministries as there are gifted people, and everyone is gifted' (*Intercom* Nov 86, 'Lay-Gifts for Ministry' by Damian Killen).

This responsibility will encourage young people to belong, give support to them, challenge others, and help them realise that they are *co-creators* of this world with God. In this climate, I wonder would the harvesters be so few?

Questions
1. What do you understand by the word 'community'? Where and how do you experience community?
2. Does any group in which you are involved, have all or some of the 'elements' outlined in this article?
3. What can you do to build 'community'? What would you need to make this happen?

Justice

by Tony Flynn

I am 22 years of age, a native of Waterford, now working with a Pharmaceutical Company in Cork.

I have always had some interest in the Third World but did not develop this until I was in third and fourth year in college. I began to learn more about injustice in general; also, I became involved in different Church-related groups, the first being Young Christian Students (YCS). Gradually I began to link the two areas together and come to an understanding of how my faith as a christian/catholic involved a responsibility to be just and to work against injustice.

As I read and discovered more about Church teaching and about injustice, in the Third World and here in Ireland, I began to see contradictions between the lifestyles of most Irish Catholics, including myself, and the teaching of Jesus. For example:

- We live a life of luxury while others die of hunger.
- Our high standard of living is at least partially due to the exploitation of Third World countries.
- We treat travellers as outcasts.
- We begrudge decent social welfare benefits to those who need them etc.

At present I am struggling to remove the contradictions between my own lifestyle and the teaching of the Scriptures as exemplified by Mt 25:31-46:

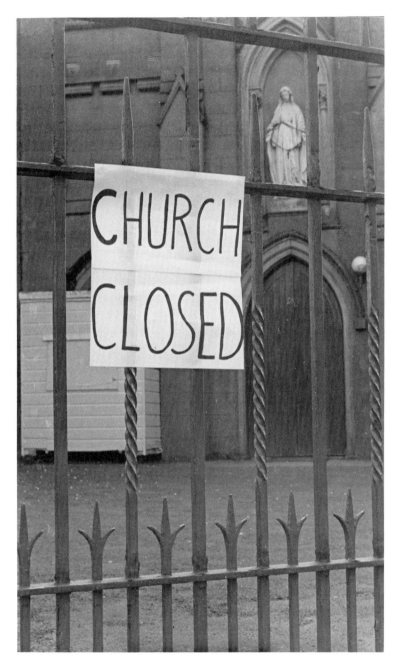

For I was hungry and you gave me food, I was thirsty and you gave me drink, I was a stranger and you made me welcome, naked and you clothed me, sick and you visited me, in prison and you came to see me.

Lord when did we see you hungry and feed you, or thirsty and give you a drink? When did we see a stranger and make you welcome, naked and clothed you, sick or in prison and go and see you?

I tell you solemnly, in so far as you did this to one of the least of these brothers or sisters of mine, you did it to me.

And Jas 2:14-18:

Take the case, my bothers and sisters of someone who has never done a single good act but claims he/she has faith. Will that faith save him/her? If one of the brothers or one of the sisters is in need of clothes and has not enough food to live on, and one of you says to them, 'I wish you well, keep yourself warm and eat plenty', without giving them these bare necessities of life, then what good is that? Faith is like that; if good works do not go with it, it is quite dead *(adapt. Jerusalem Bible popular edition)*.

Part 1: The Present

When I look around at the Ireland of today, I see two different groups of people: those who have enough to lead 'comfortable' lives, the majority; and those who lead deprived lives due to various factors including unemployment, inadequate social welfare benefits, lack of education, etc, the minority. While the latter suffer from injustice in some form, the former are happy with their own lot, and though expressing concern about the plight of the others, don't care enough to do anything about it.

Therefore when it comes to elections the comfortable think of their own pockets first, which means that parties advocating tax cuts will probably get more votes than those who support increased social welfare benefits. These types of attitudes also carry over into the area of Third World concern.

Many people in Ireland are 'charitable' and 'generous' when it comes to giving money to the Third World. However, for most people this money is what is left over when they already have most of the things they want, e.g. a car, house, central heating, wall-to-wall carpets, foreign holidays or new outfits of clothes etc. Not many people are prepared to reduce their standard of living so as to share what they have with those who have nothing.

It seems to me that the commitment of many Irish people to justice falters when some personal sacrifice is called for. For example, the Dunnes Stores strike – there was a good deal of public sympathy for the strikers, but how many people who could afford to do so actually stopped shopping in Dunnes Stores? Action speaks louder than words!

When I look at the Catholic Church which most Irish people claim to belong to, I see an institutional church whose organisation is built not on love or justice but on power. The majority of the people (i.e. the laity) have no say in the running of this institutional church. They may be referred to and 'consulted' but they are usually expected to do what they're told. A minority of people find fulfillment and responsibility in some of the many small groups that have emerged within the Church.

Also, I see a wealthy church with a large income, owning large amounts of property. I see a church which seems to place more emphasis on providing an excellent education for the rich and well-off than trying to provide even a rudimentary education for people from deprived backgrounds for whom the education system does not cater at present.

What do Irish Catholics hear their Church saying from the parish pulpit or in public statements from the hierarchy? They are regularly told to pray, go to Mass, say the Rosary, not to use contraceptives, not to engage in pre-marital sex, to vote against divorce and of course to 'love your neighbour'. However, they rarely hear sermons on unemployment, attitudes towards the travellers, inadequate social welfare benefits, or about the fact that high standards of living in this country are partly due to exploitation of Third World countries.

It appears to me that the Irish Church preaches selectively, giving very little emphasis to the social teachings of the Church. The result of this is that most church-going catholics know next to nothing about the Church's teaching on social justice, human rights or Third World issues. Indeed, many people turn away from the Church because they think its teaching has no relevance to the modern world.

All the above does not detract from the fact that there are many people both within and outside the Church who are very concerned about and are working for justice. This includes people who work with Trócaire, Gorta, Concern, Amnesty International, Simon, Unemployed Action and sections of the trade union movement.

Many individuals also contribute including some politicians, e.g. Noel Browne and Jim Kemmy. However, many of these are operating in a vacuum, i.e. either people do not accept what they are saying or, if they do, they generally give only token support.

I think it would be true to say that the majority of Irish

catholics are, by and large, ignorant of their responsibility as christian/catholics to do something about it. Because of human selfishness, many people, even though they are aware of the need, and their responsibility to help, are often very reluctant to make the sacrifices of time, money etc. which may be required.

I was hungry and you gave me to eat
I was thirsty and you gave me to drink

Part 2: The Future

How can Irish Catholics be made aware of the many injustices that exist and of their responsibility to combat them? Educational programmes are needed which would include the following three areas:

1. The extent and causes of injustice both at home and internationally.
2. The teaching of the Catholic Church on political, economic and social justice.
3. The scriptural basis for action for justice.

Different channels can be used to implement these programmes, e.g. sermons at Mass, statements by the hierarchy, religious education classes in schools, parish-based social action groups. The aim of the programmes would be to provide an understanding of the sources of injustice as well as the motivation to tackle them.

It would be essential to emphasise specific actions which could be taken by the individuals/groups who are participating in the programme. In this regard I think that parish/small groups could play a very important role as they can provide the support, motivation and resources which encourage people to act. Without the support of a group, individuals can often feel very isolated and intimidated by both the extent of injustice and the hostile/non-understanding attitude of many people.

Also, I see the need for a pamphlet/book which would state the Church's teaching on justice, drawing from papal encyclicals, speeches, conference reports, etc. A simple yet comprehensive statement would be a great asset in informing people as well as removing the many doubts and misconceptions people have regarding the Church's teaching in the area.

Questions
1. Is it possible to justify a life of comparative luxury while there is so much poverty in the world?
2. How can I as a christian/catholic live in a system, which exploits people in this country and in the Third World, without trying to change it?
3. How can more Irish people be made aware of the injustices that exist and of their responsibility to work for justice?
4. What role should the Catholic Church in Ireland be taking in the struggle for justice?

Liturgy...not just a barrage of words

by Mick Peelo

When I think of the Liturgy, what it means and its significance, an old film called 'The Time Machine' immediately comes to mind. Briefly, the film is about cannibalism. A group of cannibals have control over a particular society. They don't interfere with the ordinary everyday lives of the people. In fact, they make sure that everybody has what they want and need. However, at a certain time each day a bell rings; as soon as it is sounded, men, women and children suddenly drop everything and walk silently, as if hypnotised, into a huge tunnel. Inside, the people line up to be chosen for the cannibal's next meal. The fortunate ones leave after the picking ceremony is over and return to life outside. That society has all the appearances of a paradise . . . until the bell rings.

I'm not sure if the analogy is all that clear to you. During Sundays and other holy days of obligation one can see the masses traipse mindlessly into many large tunnels all over the country. Why? Certainly not to be chosen for the slaughter. Why then? The books and theologians tell us it is to celebrate their faith in a loving God who sent her son to redeem us from sin. What do the masses themselves say?

The weekend in Teach Bríde was an attempt to bring

young people together from different social and intellectual backgrounds with various levels of religious commitment, i.e. some of the masses, with a view to discussing their experiences of Church. Early on in the weekend the participants chose seven areas of Church life that they wanted to discuss. One of these areas was Liturgy, Worship and Prayer. I don't intend to write a report of what was said on the above theme, nor do I claim to represent anybody but myself. This article is simply a personal reflection from one of the many 'mindless' people who is at present struggling with the whole question of liturgy today. I am twenty-seven years old, a student of theology and married. I have been actively involved with liturgy and liturgical celebrations for the past six years. Of course, you'll then say that I'm not 'mindless', but I still traipse into those tunnels and each time come out wondering why I ever went in there in the first place.

Why do I keep returning to the tunnel when I know I'm only going to end up frustrated and angry? I suppose it is because I believe in liturgy and have a vision of how it could be celebrated. What I see at any given Sunday liturgy are hundreds of people but little or no communication between them, perhaps simply a nod or a handshake. Yes, prayers are recited and songs are sung, but I think it has to be said that very few of the community gathered actively participate in the liturgy, nor do they want to. In my opinion, what is essential in any liturgy is that a group of believers come together *willingly* to pray, to talk, to give thanks, to laugh, to remember, to share experiences, to tell stories, to listen and to celebrate by praising, dancing, singing, etc. The Eucharist is one such liturgy. Here one of the believers, specially called and chosen, presides at a celebration that is central to the faith and mission of the Church. At this assembly stories are told to remind us of our history – they open up our past giving us a sense of where we have come from. These stories should throw light on our own life-stories, giving them direction and meaning. Here too, we are reminded of what we are called to become.

The Eucharist is a political statement. It is political because of its nature, it draws people together for a common purpose. It is political because it calls us to adopt values that are very often contrary to the consumerist, materialistic values of our present society. The Eucharist demands that we become political people because ultimately it is concerned with changing human beings and societies. As believers, our part in this process is to be instruments of that change.

Liturgy reflects the faith, hope and love of the community. It is a sharing of their common faith, a sign and expression of their hope in the Kingdom and its values, and a celebration of their mutual love and support for each other in bringing about this Kingdom. Liturgies then, are dynamic celebrations involving, and belonging to, the whole community, for without the community no liturgy could take place.

What I have expressed here is not the reality is it? It is not easy to portray the reality without sounding dismissive, frustated, impatient, angry or anti-clerical, but these are real feelings I possess when faced with the liturgy as it is presently conducted.

When I come out of the tunnel I inevitably hear people talk about what happened inside. Some refer to the liturgy as if it were a film, others don't talk about it at all. My own reflections tend to follow the former. The conclusion to be drawn from this is that liturgy has become something apart from us, outside us – a spectacle to be observed and later forgotten. It was never intended to be this way. It no longer belongs to the people. We must claim ownership and responsibility for it. In this way liturgy can become a relevant and true celebration, of the community, in a word *ours*.

share
experiences
pray
tell stories
talk
laugh
listen
remember
sing
dance

Because of the way liturgies are structured and organised there is no possible way that we could make them ours even if we wanted to. Firstly, there are too many people. There's no room for sharing, no room for telling our faith stories or listening to each other. This tends to high-light an individualistic approach to our faith – God and me and nobody else. Secondly, the language used is not the people's language. It is highly theological and mysterious. It pre-supposes a particular understanding of God and faith that is often outside people's experience, and thus it is irrelevant and meaningless. The language, because it is sexist, creates and maintains a patriarchal institution. Unfortunately, this language is fixed, it has power over people but they have little or no opportunity to change it. Thirdly, liturgy is owned by the clergy. They have complete power over an essential aspect of church life that should be the responsibility of the local community. Whether they have been given this power or have taken it is beside the point, the fact remains that liturgy is imposed on us by the clergy, our part in it is only incidental. The second Vatican Council called for a fuller, more active participation in the liturgy on the part of the laity, but participation is just a token gesture in an event that is going to take place regardless of whether the people are present or not. Liturgies have become static, locked in the past, controlled by the clergy and thus, in my view, have lost their significance.

I have had to stop going back for more. I would be only fooling myself and others if I did go. For me it is not a celebration nor is it a prayer and I have the feeling that many people have similar experiences of liturgy but make their prayer one of resignation to grin and bear it. I'm not sure if that's adequate. If my analysis and criticism of the liturgy is sound and true to our experience, then we should do something about it. If our congregations are too large then we need to form smaller communities that lend themselves to constructive communication. If the language is beyond us and also sexist we should bring it alive by using our own words and experiences, keeping in mind the many traditions from which our Christianity has drawn. Some of these traditions may need to be re-examined and developed and this is where we need discussion and expertise. Finally, if we worship together in smaller groups and modify our language accordingly we should find that the liturgy will become our celebration. Here, the priesthood of the people of God is visible in the community ministering to one another. The priest, the one called and chosen among the believers to preside at the Eucharist, exercises the gift of priesthood rather than the clerical office.

Over the past two years or so I have tried, with a few others, to make this alternative a reality. What is called for is a complete structural overhaul and those maintaining the structure certainly won't want to change it. So who will?

You may have noticed I have been using the image of a tunnel to refer to what is more commonly called a 'Church'. The reason is that I feel we have been confusing our terminology. We, the people, are the Church. If we continually refer to the building we worship in as a Church it will eventually become more important than us, the people. When St Paul spoke about the Church at Corinth he was not referring to the building. Anyway, for my purposes the tunnel image has been a useful one. However, we need to find another term for our houses of worship, or clarify the existing terminology.

Nothing new has been said in this article, but progress is only made by saying and doing the old things over and over again in a new and dynamic way that speaks to the present. I have little confidence in the written word as an effective instrument of change, but I suppose that depends on where it falls, or where it is sown.

By the way, 'The Time Machine' ends with the hero (as usual) destroying the cannibals and their tunnel and thereby liberating the people from that dreadful tyranny, enabling them to take responsibility for their own lives. Funny, that hero reminds me of another great liberator!

Questions
1. What is your experience of liturgy, be it baptism, a prayer meeting, a Eucharist, a funeral?
2. Does 'participation' mean that we become priests, readers, ministers of the Eucharist, members of the

choir or folk group, or is it essentially something more than this?

3. 'It is no longer a sin if you miss Mass on Sundays and Holydays'. Imagine if the bishops came out with some such statement. What would your reaction be? What, do you think, would be the reactions of the other Mass-goers?

4. How do you think the liturgy could be improved in your own parish? What part could you play in bringing about that change?

A prayer to the God of justice

My God of justice:
today I met a man by the beach,
who asked me
if you had winced
when Lucy, who is three,
was washed up on the shore,
and I said you had.

Sally-Anne who is 32,
and works from street lamps,
looked at me through mascara eyes
and asked me if you cry
when you feel her pain.
I said you do.

Peter's instruments of peace
are a needle, spoon and flame,
and once he said he believed,
and asked me if you still do,
and I said you do.

For you, my God of justice,
could not instill in me the power to feel,
if you knew not how to, yourself.
So I think you cry and wince,
at the injustice inflicted by our hands and hearts.
Yes, I'm sure you do.

Dearbhla McArdle

"For us women & for our salvation...."

by Toni Walsh

The idea of 'women in the Church' must conjure up many different images for people. For some it may be an image of beautiful flower arrangements and shiny altar rails, for others it may be angelic renditions of 'Soul of my Saviour' from the organ loft, for others still it could be religious orders of sisters, and so on. For me it provokes feelings – feelings of pain and frustration, of anger and weariness, of alienation and oppression.

Twenty four years ago I was baptised into the Roman Catholic Church, a church whose catholicity is sadly lacking in its failure to embrace and listen to all God's people. However, I have chosen to remain a part of this broken institution and to use my energy as positively and creatively as possible. In case this energy should dissipate completely I have decided to put the following few thoughts together. What I write is my own experience as a woman who is trying to live out the implications of baptism. I don't intend to either modify or apologise for the anger that permeates my bones as I write. I am weary of 'channelling passion' for fear of being dismissed as an irate young woman who 'is really having problems with her faith – God love her'! Often when someone criticises the Church they are accused of 'clergy bashing'. I intend to present reality as I see it – if verbalising the truth 'bashes' anybody then maybe they deserved to be 'bashed'!

Throughout this reflection I will be referring to 'Church' mainly as institution.

Women are probably the most dynamic force in society today. Yet the Church, a very powerful structure, is choosing not to tap this dynamism. I would go a step further and say that it is choosing to ignore it. In my ten years of involvement in the Church I have come in contact with many groups, e.g. folk groups, Christian communities, prayer groups, church action groups – women constituted a vast percentage of the personnel. A parallel can be made with the Irish workforce where women make up eighty percent or more of the labour force, in the category of service workers, but only three percent of the executives and managers in industry[1]. No need to ask who holds the 'executive' jobs in the Church!

At this point I would like to clarify something that may have entered your head. I am not promoting, demoting, suggesting or hinting at anything to do with the ordination of women. That is a separate issue entirely. To presume that the question of priesthood is *the* primary concern is a total misrepresentation of the vision and spirit of women. Must women be ordained in order to minister? For me, this slights and undermines the role of the non-ordained, i.e. laity, and calls for an awakening and a greater understanding of the priesthood of the people, another question for another time.

The Church, like society, is a patriarchal institution and has been so down through the years. Power is taken and held by a small group comprised only of men. As tradition is sacred (is it?), and is to be respected (more than people?), this pattern has remained with us into the broad-minded, equality-loving eighties! But is there justice in propogating and protecting a patriarchal structure that excludes fifty percent of the population? Is this the kind of morality that the Church wishes to promote? One would expect that those who are involved in discerning, reflecting, conscientising and, dare I say it, praying, would have enough insight to see that something is terribly wrong.

Women have never been encouraged or invited to be a part of the decision-making process of the Church, 'a Church where it is common practice for celibates to speak for the married, for men to speak for women, for bishops to speak for the laity'[2]. As a gesture of good-will women are permitted to be active in the Church in a cosmetic way – a tokenistic involvement that gives a good PR image. At present, the participation of women is dependent on and determined by a group of men known as the clergy. That anyone's active participation in the Church is determined by a select group of men is a disgrace and an embarassment. An example of blatant discrimination against women is Canon 230 of the Code of Canon Law, which implies that laywomen cannot become permanent lectors or acolytes: (1) Lay *men* whose age and talents meet the requirements by decree of the Episcopal Conference can be given the *stable ministry* of lector and of acolyte, through the prescribed liturgical rite . . . (2) Lay *people* can receive a *temporary assignment* to the role of lector in liturgical actions – a woman's contribution is at the mercy of a parish priest or local bishop!

Perhaps less subtle is the oppressiveness of the language employed by the institutional Church, particularly in the area of communal worship. I have been surprised at the number of people who consider language to be superficial and even neutral. However, I feel confident enough to state that language creates, that language conditions, and that language is exclusive:

When we use words we draw pictures, set scenes, fire

the imaginations of those who listen. We do this un-
consciously by our choice of words – hence the
creativity of language. If we listen to something which
is repeated over and over again we will eventually accept the images being created by the words – hence
the conditioning power of language. If I decide to ad-
dress myself to women only as I write this article then I
will exclude the non-female readership – hence the
exclusiveness of language.

Eucharistic Prayer IV is a perfect example of this
threefold power of language at work in our Eucharistic
celebration, as was demonstrated at the workshop
weekend in Teach Bríde:

  . . . You formed man in your own likeness and set him
  over the whole world to serve you, his creator, and to
  rule over all creatures . . .

As is obvious, the image created here is predominantly
male. 'Man' is powerful. 'Man' is like God. Is God like
'man' – male? The more often we hear these words the
more conditioned we become, conditioned into accepting passively the male 'stamp' on our faith, conditioned
to the point of not even noticing that someone is being
excluded.

As I almost numbly chant the words of the Creed I cannot help grinning to myself at the stupidity of me, a
woman, saying: '. . . for us men and for our salvation . . .'! On the one hand there is an acknowledgement
of this improper use of language; for example, the word
'men' may now be omitted from the Prayer of Consecra-
tion: 'it will be shed for you and for all (men) . . .'. But
on the other hand, we are being told that the words man,
men, mankind, etc embrace both genders. So for some of
the time it is very wrong to use sexist terminology but at
other times it is acceptable – a bit inconsistent in my

Excludes Conditions

Oppresses

Creates

Challenges

Language

view! Terms such as Father, Kingdom, Mankind, Sonship, Brethren, Fellowship, etc, have been passed to us unquestioned, but the time has come for questioning. Surely growth and development are about review, honest discernment and change. Our words should be an outward expression of an inner depth, not a source of controversy.

There is little biblical or theological evidence to justify a male dominated Church. Women were obviously very much a part of Christ's discipleship. Nothing can refute the claim that women were present at the institution of the Eucharist. But tradition, moulded by the patriarchal potter has superceded the truth, and the lived reality has become smeared by the ugliness of power – a human weakness which has infiltrated all institutionalised aspects of life.

I see little hope of change in the hierarchical ranks of our Church, a sad admission which I would prefer not to believe. As long as there is a preoccupation with buildings, laws, finance, status, influence, clericalism etc, there will never be room for the life experiences of people. For most, the Church is an irrelevant body which is in constant contradiction of itself. Some keep plodding until they realise that there is a certain threshold of involvement beyond which non-ordained people cannot tread. At that stage many turn their backs and go and others continue to carry the cross of 'layhood'. I have often turned to go but something has called me back each time, a vision maybe, of a Church which is community, a Church which is women and men together, a Church which is in touch with the authentic spirit of Christ, and which is committed to the eradication of sexual apartheid among other tools of oppression.

Questions

1. What is sexual apartheid?
   Where do you see it in action?
2. God is a woman. Discuss.
3. Find other examples of sexist language. Analyse them, discuss them. Put them into non-sexist form.
4. Look for references and stories about women in the bible. How are women portrayed? Who, for you, is the most significant/interesting woman? Why?
5. What is the role of men in the liberation of women?

Notes:

1. Sources:
   (a) 'Lifting the Lid', Handbook of facts and information on Ireland by Ursula Barry (Attic Press, 1986).
   (b) 'Women in the Labour Force', by John Blackwell (Employment Equality Agency, 1986).
2. 'Who Speaks for the Laity?', by Ben Kimmerling, *The Furrow*, Vol 37. No 9. September, 1986.

Power
to Empower

by Kieran Byrne

To find a way to begin *this* reflection, I needed a password. It had to be 'power'. It seems when relating to structures we experience either power or the lack of it (powerlessness). But what is power? It would take a great deal more than this reflection allows to define power accurately, but clearly those who have power feel they can do; can influence; and have effect. The powerless feel ineffectual, that what they have to offer is useless. Almost all of those involved in the weekend workshop in Teach Bríde expressed this in one form or another. Sadly the predominant experience among these young people is a bitter powerlessness in relation to the official Church and its structures – no room for diversity; no real support in developing skills and knowledge; no forum of communication; oppressive language; apparent irrelevance of ordinary human experience. When you take on this 'structure' it feels like David facing Goliath.

But let us look deeper. Surely structures, like any frameworks, in themselves are not necessarily harmful. After all we need them to organise ourselves around our common Christian aim. But *are our* structures themselves Christian? What form do they take? The early Christian church began structure-less and only once organisation was needed did it adopt structures. From the experience of many it would seem that Church as 'people' has laid down with institutionalism as a structural form. Institutionalism is an extreme form where the governing elements, the visible structure, becomes of *primary* importance. It is this institutionalism that breeds much of what we experience in the context of Church. What was once perhaps a means to a Christian end is now the end in itself. Has maintenance of the institution become our primary and perverted aim? Let us look at the features that are visible and the values behind them might become clearer.

The feature of order
Institutionalism needs officers to protect itself. We have bought into clericalism and a hierarchy. We see ordered roles where every Catholic knows her or his own place rigidly in the scheme of things. Clericalism is like a specialised order within that controls the way things are – teaching and governing; decision making; even about what is sacred and what is not, this all remains with the few (it happens to be men – or does it just happen?). This, of course, breeds passivity – even dependence where we, both cleric and lay, become incapable of making an independent decision and it seems, also incapable of taking independent action. Active participation in the running of things remains for the most part with the few. Even the gestures towards 'lay involvement' e.g. ministries of the Eucharist and the Word, are at best tokenism and may even perpetuate clericalism by adding 'pseudo clerics' to its ranks in some cases. Are lay people being invited to join a clerical, institutionalised Church? Surely the lay-cleric dichotomy is misleading, even false! Before we rush to blame it all on the clergy, let us remember that by silent, passive response or by a non-decision to change things, we are in fact, lending support

to this structure, the one that sees those governing as primary. Surely we, the clerics and the laity, are all in this together?

The feature of the law
Institutionalism draws on legalism in order to protect itself. *Legalism* is more interested in the letter of the law than in the spirit out of which it was created. A right and wrong, black and white approach to things with built-in punishment. The result is that morality is reduced to keeping rules and laws (who makes them?) instead of *real* commitment to *real* unleashed, Christian values e.g. a struggle and search for what is good. Again we (cleric and lay) succumb to this seduction because it suits us; we need not claim any responsibility for our behaviour, individual or collective – it's all done for us. Ultimately responsibility moves upward in a hierarchical system. But look at what it does – we become obedient to humans (mostly men) and not to God!

Strengths
Institutionalism as a structural form, of course, has strengths that commend it to us. Firstly, it is international, well defined with strong claims to divine revelation, its dogma and government are rich in content, e.g. strong scholarly tradition. Secondly, in a time when there is rapid change and 'progress' (shifting sands), many suffer from 'future shock', the inability to cope with quick changes. An institution that has a powerful and esteemed past is like a much needed anchor or armchair, e.g. the recent return to novenas and parish missions as devotional forms. Thirdly, the strong corporate identity within Catholicism is security in insecure times, is stability and continuity within pluralism (where difference and not sameness is valued).

Weaknesses

The Church as prophet almost disappears. To be prophetic means to be 'anti-structure', not in the sense of being against all structures but rather to be critical and suspicious in order to keep them pure and free from injustice. This has always been one of the strongest elements of Christianity and Jesus' ministry. The prophet mourns the death of the old order of things because of his or her own vested interests in keeping it alive. The prophet stands to lose part of his or herself. Then, the prophet announces the arrival of the new order by living as though it is here. Jesus lived the Kingdom which *is* certainly anti-structure in that it turns things as we know them upside-down. Institutionalism needs to expel prophecy to survive. We see this today in the many who have criticised but have not been heard or valued. Some are even cut off, amputated.

Institutionalism which needs sameness has only meagre basis in scripture or tradition. Uniformity in living styles, corporateness in organisation is not a strong feature of scripture even in the early church where diversity and multi-giftedness were highly valued. Institutionalism does not allow for people to be different.

Because the teaching within our Church is assumed and sanctioned by the few, much of our theology, analysis, methods etc are uncreative, sometimes oppressive, e.g. liturgy and the role of women, sexist language. They reflect a narrow human experience (usually a clerical experience which is mostly middleclass).

Institutionalism is narrow and exclusive and not open to other traditions and their ideas – difference is difficult. Ecumenism stands little chance.

The institutionalised Church stands outside of history. It stands outside because it does not deal with the real lived experiences, concerns or needs of the people, e.g. unemployment, emmigration etc. As such the Church remains staunch and naive – a castle in the air. In Ireland the main concern of the official Church seems to be sexual morality and not unemployment or poverty.

Institutionalism breeds individualism – a totally personalised and isolated 'me and my God' faith. Responsibility in faith and action remains personal and rarely shared in any real way. Many young people have noted on leaving the Church that no-one really noticed.

1 becoming we

It seems that we, lay and cleric, have managed to divide our Church, polarise it into the powerful and the powerless. The image of a supermarket comes to me, each of us pushing our own trolleys down predetermined aisles. In building structures we are dealing with power and freedom. Who has the power? Those who control areas of uncertainty; those who make rules and functions; those with the skills and competence; those who control information. How can the Church empower all of its people? How do we build a structure that is just and includes rather than excludes, one that is true to the Christian vision? 'My mother and brothers are those who hear the word of God and obey it' (Lk 8:21).

A beginning

The image that I would find most helpful is that of the 'body'. The skeleton, the frame, is the last part to be formed in the womb but upon which so much depends. Our skeletons are built so that we can adapt, grow and learn.

It is, however, the flesh, the muscle, the heart and the mind that decides. Surely structure must be like this, dynamic and yet dependent on the experience of the flesh for growth. We must adjust the collective action, the shared action, coming from lived experience to meet the original and still vital aims of Christianity, the Kingdom. Real change will only take place if we all change.

In short, it seems a structure would need to contain at least the following elements:

- The units need to be *small* so that community can grow more easily, a situation where people are known and can belong. Furthermore, adaptability to change when needed is less sluggish in a smaller group. When small it is more likely that skills and resources will be more easily recognised and used.

- There would need to be built-in, on-going *reflection* on *action*.

- Human *experience* needs to be the source of the life of the Church. This would place the Church within the real needs and concerns of the people, e.g. how little we have listened to the experience of women, how often we have ignored and oppressed all that is feminine?

- The structure needs to include and value its *prophets* – those who question the way things are and the presumptions of the status quo; those who live anti-structurally.

- The structure must move from an 'I' to a 'We' consciousness.

- The structure must enable us to be immersed with those powerless, voiceless marginalised ones in society. 'He has chosen me to bring good news to the poor' (Lk 4:18).

When looking at the Church in Ireland, we would have to be suspicious of the structures it has employed to organise itself. We are immediately confronted with the imbalance in people's capacity to exercise power. In fact, the Church not only maintains itself but also the status quo throughout society by ignoring issues of inequality like unemployment, women's issues etc. The Church instead of a sign of God is a sign of, a reflection of, the status quo. In order to find a structure that best facilitates the Christian vision, we must root our experience and our reflection on it in the Gospels – realising that the gospels when preached within an institutionalised structure only succeed in keeping us powerless. But we could release the radical and subversive power by telling the stories and allowing them to mingle with the very issues that face our lives. We then would go to the gospels, not cold, hoping for illumination, but hot from our daily struggles about issues of powerlessness to find a new meaning and direction. Empowering the most marginalised in Ireland – e.g. travellers, single parents, unemployed – becomes one with the liberation revealed through Jesus Christ in the gospels. 'I was hungry and you fed me, thirsty and you gave me a drink . . .' (Mt 25).

Questions
1. What is your experience of the Church and its structures, including your local parish?
2. In your experience of Church:
   Who is powerful?
   Who is powerless?
   Who benefits?
   Who does not benefit?
3. What would you wish to see different?
4. What would have to happen for things to be different?
5. What can you do to effect real change?

For those who care to remember
After a while, she would leave,
But not before the dull ache, in her knees,
became too much to bear.
Her fingers passed over worn, wooden beads
for maybe the thousandth time,
and in odd moments
she would touch and kiss the tiny crucifix
and mutter incoherent words to herself or 'him'.
Her mind, as always, would drift back
over thirty or more years,
of which half, it seemed, were spent
in this dark, safe, sanctuary
that on July's hottest day
was cold and damp
always untouched by sunshine.

She thought of little Johnny
Who, on a mid-March rainy Sunday,
Looked back out through the door of this place
and said, 'it's pissin' Ma'.
God, she thought she would die that day,
and she swore she'd hammer him
when she got home – but she didn't.
He was gone now,
Rarely there to share the memories,
so, in this safe place,
she would share them with herself and 'him'
the eternal listener,
and after a while
she would leave
and re-enter a world,
a world far smaller than her own.

Dearbhla McArdle

Working together?

by Paula Goggin

The weekend in Teach Bríde functioned on many different levels – it was different things for many people. I was a member of the team, one of a group of eight people who facilitated the weekend. Consequently my reflections on the weekend will be more concerned with how things were done and why than with what was said by the group.

I preface all my thoughts and reflections with the belief that the weekend was worthwhile. It was at times exciting, at times tense; it held within it many conflicts, grievances and situations which bore an uncanny resemblance to my own experience of Church. The weekend saw much discussion about *power,* the power of the Church, the power of the clergy, the powerlessness of some in relation to the Church. However, it was also a weekend where 'power' came into operation and was called into question at many levels. 'Power' is not a negative word, it is the use of power that is either positive or negative. Both were experienced during the weekend in the inter-action of team members with each other, with the group etc.

Teamwork, is a concept that has been allowed to gather several vague meanings. It does not mean 'we'll all muck in together', or 'one way or another we'll get things done', not effective teamwork in any case. It involves a group of people working together towards a common purpose. It involves allowing difference where it means finding a better way. At the beginning of the weekend the team were briefed on the aim and purpose of the weekend. This aim was modified as we progressed, but it was a common point from which we all worked.

In a team, each member must be clear on her/his role and that of each of the other members. Having clearly defined roles does not exclude inter-action; on the contrary it leads to more fruitful teamwork. Clear role definition does not necessarily mean hierarchy as it seems to in Church structures. Hierarchy and teamwork are mutually exclusive. The team for the weekend suffered, I think, from a slight case of role confusion or rather, ill defined roles. This became obvious during team meetings, of which there were many, and hindered a great deal of the smooth running of the meetings. In fact, the overall facilitator of the weekend was the only one with a clearly defined role. This phenomenon can also be seen in the Church: the hierarchy have clearly defined roles, albeit questionable, but nevertheless, clearly defined. What of the laity?

The process used by the team at meetings seems to have been a little ill defined. I could not label it with any degree of certainty. At times the process seemed to work on the assumption of defined roles existing in the team, but for the most part these did not exist. Personal feelings often intruded and hindered progress. The process used fluctuated between addressing the professional roles of each member and placating the personalities in the group. This will not work. Team meetings were sometimes tense, and often resulted in conflict. The conflict itself was not undesirable, or necessarily bad, but when conflict leads nowhere and only results in hurt feelings it is fruitless. This kind of conflict only saps energy and renders dialogue and inter-action almost impossible. On the other hand, fruitful conflict or disagreement, in the context of our common purpose, is basically good, especially when it leads to a clearer vision, or to a better way of doing things. This conflict can be handled with a professionalism that goes beyond the personal in order for the system to work as it should. This does not mean to exclude the personal but rather to channel feelings etc in a constructive fashion with a view to common purpose. For any group to work together effectively towards a common vision, dialogue and inter-action are essential. From a young lay-person's point of view these are notably absent in the Church; for example, the consultation with the laity in relation to the forthcoming Synod was aptly termed 'deliberation without consultation' by Resource Magazine.

For a group to engage in dialogue and inter-action they must be prepared for difficulty and conflict. It is not easy but it is worthwhile. That group will also experience the benefit of a fuller and more representative vision or way of doing things.

However, while our teamwork was far from the ideal, it was equally distant from the abyssmal. We worked hard as a group, constantly striving for what was the best way to do things for the total group.

The journey is as important as the destination

Working on the team was a stimulating and exciting experience. The weekend and the process used demanded much. It was a challenge that was well met by many. The process used in the larger group was highly task orientated, because it had to be. This was difficult for many. Many people seemed unaccustomed to working hard towards a goal in the context of a weekend on 'Church'. This tells its own story. I feel that, to a large extent, young people have been conditioned into believing that their involvement in Church is inactive and merely a matter of passive assent or dissent.

The group was required to cover a lot of ground during the weekend both in small group situations and in the larger group. They responded well to this and good work was done. This process demanded that team members act as facilitators in the small groups. We needed to be able to lead, yet not intrude or unduly influence. This is a very difficult task, a skill that not everyone has naturally. If people are to be actively involved in the Church then they need training and education in the necessary skills. However, the members of the team, for the most part, rose admirably to the challenge. It was difficult, at times frustrating, verging on the impossible.

I mentioned power at the beginning of this article. I use it now with reference to the entire group. We held power, power to include or exclude. As a group, we excluded some people throughout the weekend through our use of language. Language became a barrier instead of an open door, a meeting place. But we also struggled to include in the small group situation, to hear and to listen to all, to represent all. This was not always successful, and by the end of the weekend it was clear that not all were represented, that some were voiceless. There existed a forum for many; in the ideal it was for all. But those who used it comfortably were those who were able to articulate dissent or agreement. To discover that we had excluded some people, albeit unwittingly, was not a pleasant experience. The struggle to include all, and yet not to descend into condescension was frustrating, exasperating, difficult and worthwhile. It was a humbling experience to find oneself in a group of people criticising the Church for its inherent inequality, and at the same time rendering some in the group voiceless, oppressed, unequal. This experience bore many resemblances to my own experience of Church and gave me new insights: this experience is also exciting and difficult, frustrating and worthwhile – a dynamic process.

To allow diversity is a demand placed upon the Church by the young, especially those present at the weekend. It must be said that in the end, the group experienced at first hand the difficulty of this demand. We coped very badly with difference and were not aware enough of its existence – or at least did little to show it. However, the diversity made itself felt and had to be acknowledged. The group was allowed the healthy opportunity of seeing itself fail in what they so ardently demanded of the Church.

It was a weekend in which much was said and thought. Many diverse opinions were gathered and held together as far as possible. What struck me most forcibly about what was voiced by the group, was the over-whelmingly negative view of our catholic tradition held by young people. I believe there are good things in our tradition which are often over-looked. Young people need to be educated towards viewing more positively their catholicism.

As a team we maintained our committment to a common purpose, although often we were in danger of losing our way. Teamwork is not easy, but I believe it is worthwhile. Though it may pose a threat to many within the Church, the step must be taken for progress to take place.

Finally, I must say I thoroughly enjoyed the weekend. It was exciting, tiring, stimulating and most of all worthwhile. It was an opportunity to work with a group of people who were committed to the weekend and to the Church. I learned much about group inter-action and working on a team. I was reaffirmed in the belief that I can contribute and work towards change within the Church, and in the knowledge that we need to learn to work together.

Questions
1. Consider how we can use power to include or to exclude when we work with others.
2. Think of ways in which you could begin to use teamwork in your local Church situation.
3. Processes used by a group when working together must always be clearly defined. Critically examine a process which you may have used. *Note:* One is not always aware that one is using a process.

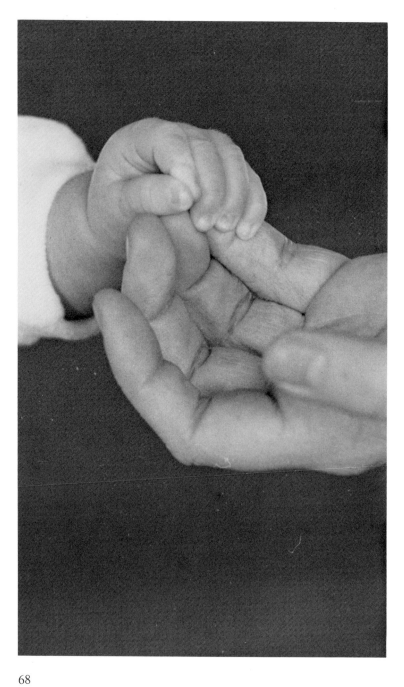

The end of the Yellow Brick Road

by Bishop Donal Murray

The reflections on the weekend in Teach Bríde reveal an intense awareness of the fact that the world is in urgent need of the Gospel message. There is impatience at injustice, unemployment and discrimination which threaten human dignity; there is readiness to play a part in building a world of justice, love and peace; there is anger at all that is seen as standing in the way of that goal.

All this is welcome, even exhilarating; but there is something missing.

It has been said that the role of young people in any society is to see all that is wrong and to denounce it as intolerable. The role of older people is to say, 'Yes, but *how* do we change it? Have you thought about *these* snags? Where will the money come from?' Neither the creative indignation nor the practical realism can be disregarded. Without the former there is only stagnation; without the latter there is only wasted and misdirected energy. The generations need each other. It is only through a dialogue where each group honestly and unapologetically makes its own contribution that real progress can be made. If that is true, then my role is to say 'Yes, but . . .'

It is stimulating to hear the indignation. It makes one reflect as to whether some of the 'buts' that spring to mind may not be 'cop outs'. At the same time, one cannot help reflecting that the 'buts' did not get much of a hearing during the weekend!

The first 'but' concerns 'the institutional Church'. This, it seems, is seen as a structure of virtually unlimited power which obstructs the formation of small groups, which prevents people from taking initiatives in working for justice, which oppresses all and sundry, which regards women as mere tea makers and brass polishers and which is impervious to anything that lay people, young or old, might say.

There is no denying that structures are often imperfect and slow; there is no denying that those who hold office in the Church make errors of judgment and suffer from human frailties like everybody else; there is no denying that every member of the Church should be concerned with flaws in our structures, and in our lives, which diminish the effectiveness of our witness and of our activity. What must be denied if we are really to make the Gospel of Christ live in the world is that reform of Church structures should be the overriding and exclusive focus of our efforts. The truth is rather, as the Synod of Bishops put it in 1985: 'The Church becomes more credible if it speaks less about itself and more and more preaches Christ crucified and witnesses to him by its life'.

One is reminded of the Wizard of Oz. Dorothy and her friends, the brainless Scarecrow, the Tin Woodman with no heart and the cowardly Lion, set out along the Yellow Brick Road to find the Great and Terrible Wizard who would give them all they desired. At the end of the search, they found only an ordinary man with no magical powers. He had been pushed into the role of Wizard by people who felt the need of powerful magic to protect them. All that the old man's 'magic' could do was to help them recognise that they already possessed all the wisdom, the love and the courage that they needed.

The Wizard succumbed to the temptation of trying to

live up to people's unrealistic expectations: 'How can I help being a humbug when all these people make me do things that everybody knows can't be done?'[1] It was a temptation that the Apostles faced too: 'Friends, what do you think you are doing? We are only human beings like you' (Acts 14:15, cf. Acts 10:26).

When people suggest how pastoral programmes and priorities should be renewed and how structures could be improved, it is the job of priests and bishops to listen. If, however, making those suggestions provides an excuse for not tackling the issues of suffering, injustice, unbelief and shortsightedness which are all around us, it is time to ask whether this is not a form of going off to see the Wizard along the Yellow Brick Road! The wisdom, the love and the courage required to face up to crying needs are already possessed by those who claim that they can do nothing until the institution is reformed.

What precisely are the structures and the policies which *prevent* young people from carrying the Gospel into their lives and into the world? If, on the other hand, the structures simply fail to give as much encouragement and support as one would like, surely it is in the attempt to live the Gospel and to rise to the challenge that the need for improvements will emerge?

The 'yes' which goes with this first 'but' is to the idea that the Church should be seen more as a community and less as a structure. It is necessary to find ways of living as a community at all levels, from families to small groups to parishes, dioceses and the universal Church. The strange thing is that the much reviled 'institutional Church' has been saying this as loudly as it can for a long time! The final report of the Synod of Bishops (Section II, C,6)[2] could almost serve as a summary of what the participants in the Teach Bríde weekend were demanding.

What is required is not a snatching of the 'levers of power' from the unwilling hands of the bishops but a working together towards goals which we share. On this, as on many other issues, bishops can identify with the British cabinet minister who said, 'Well, here I am pulling the levers of power, and nothing is happening!'

In building up a sense of community, small groups of various kinds have a vital part to play. They can be a spur to more creative and imaginative activity, drawing out, appreciating, challenging and combining the talents of the members. They can be a forum for deeper and richer understanding of the message of Christ and the salvation he offers. They can be places of prayer and celebration of the presence of Christ in our lives. Not the least among their benefits can be a growth in the recognition of the value of the Christian efforts that people are already making in their lives and a realisation that in making these efforts they are not alone.

Much of the dissatisfaction that is expressed with regard to the liturgy can be traced to a lack of that sense. Gifts are not being fully used and, even where they are being used, they are not recognised. That is why the celebration, and even the congregation, can sometimes seem dead.

The unleashing of the Christian powers which 'are often buried and suffocated'[3] as Pope Paul VI put it, is not primarily a matter of the clergy inviting people to do things. The activity of the Christian community does not consist in doing jobs handed out by the priest. It consists in each individual, each family, each group living out its own baptismal relationship to Christ and it's mission in the world.

This leads us to the second 'but' which concerns the idea that the liturgy should express 'our' thoughts, feelings and concerns. It must be right that the People of God should be able to say, 'This is *our* liturgy'. This cannot, however, mean that it belongs to any particular group within the Church. The Sunday liturgy is the setting in which all the smaller communities and individuals should be able to recognise one another as belonging to a wider whole. The priorities and concerns of any one group do not exhaust the richness of the Gospel or of the Christian life. The parish liturgy should say to each of us that the Body of Christ in all its variety is bigger than me and my concerns. That requires an effort of understanding on the part of every participant to enter into something which is not a private celebration but is 'ours' in the fullest sense. This is not to say that there is no place for smaller groups to celebrate and reflect on their attempts to follow Christ and even, on occasion, to celebrate a group Mass. Nevertheless, without a liturgy in which all belong, any small group, however full of vitality, is liable to drift away from the unity in difference which is the mark of real community.

That wider belonging stretches to all the members of a parish; it stretches across the world to people of other cultures and languages; it stretches across history to those who followed Christ in earlier centuries and to those who will, we hope, come after us. These are the 'us' to whom the liturgy belongs.

For that reason, one must also enter a 'but' with regard to the idea that the doctrines of the Church are imposed, presumably by the bishops. We are part of a tradition which links us to Christ. Our faith is ours, but not in the sense that we can alter it as we wish. The teaching of the Church is not an arbitrary imposition; it is a living tradition. If we are not part of that tradition, we have severed our roots.

Our perspective is not the whole truth. Victor Hugo's words may serve as a warning: 'It is said that God created man in his own image; man has retaliated'. We must not create a god 'cut to the measure of western intellectuals of the dying twentieth century'[4]. We must not try to fashion a Church so tied to the 1980s that it will have nothing to offer to the twenty-first century. The Church to which we belong is richer than any one generation can exhaust or appreciate.

The 'yes' implied by these 'buts' is that the liturgy and doctrine of the Church must indeed become ours. This involves, in the first place, a process of receiving. We approach the Word of God and the tradition which has carried it to us with respect. It is something which we receive, not something which we create, though we have to be creative in order to find ways of making that message live in our day and speak to the problems and hopes of our world. A welcoming submission to the Word of God is required from bishops and the Pope no less than from lay people. 'What we preach is not ourselves but Jesus Christ as Lord' (2 Cor 4:5, cf. Vatican II, *Decree on Revelation* 7-10).

The third 'but' has to do with the role of women in the Church. The frustration that is expressed is understandable and partly justified. It must, however, be said that the history of the Church, and particularly the history of this country, would not justify the statement that women have been confined to cleaning and tea-making. The large scale of the Church's involvement in education and health care in Ireland is largely the work of women, including some very remarkable foundresses of religious orders. Today, the participation of women in the life of many parishes, as volunteer missionaries, even in the allegedly male preserve of the Commissions of the

Episcopal Conference, while it leaves room for improvement, is very considerable. If a mere man were to dismiss all of this work in the terms used by some of the writers, there would be a justifiable storm of outrage!

The problem of 'sexist' language in the liturgy is a source of irritation. Perhaps this is not so much a symptom of the ineffectiveness of the women's movement as of its remarkable success. In the space of a decade or so, the English language has been profoundly changed. While I am not entirely convinced that the use of terms like 'mankind' did in the past imply any downplaying of women any more than the use of the term geese involves a downplaying of ganders, such linguistic shortcuts have become unacceptable in an astonishingly short period of time.

Some changes to the liturgical texts have been made. The thorough revision of all the liturgical texts which is required for this and for other reasons is progressing. It involves a great deal of consultation which is a frustratingly slow process covering all the English speaking countries. One must remark, incidentally, that there is some conflict involved in demanding both more consultation and quicker decision making!

There must, of course, be a resounding 'yes' to the call that women should be more involved in the life of the Church and there must be a fuller recognition of their existing contribution.

This leads to a final 'but'. It is a little disturbing to see participation referred to so consistently in terms of 'access to decision making'. That is part of it, but it is by no means the core of it. The Church is not a business corporation; it is a community. Participating in the Church's life is not like being a member of a Board of Directors. The suggestion that every decision should be the fruit of hearing the views of every member is a call for structures which would be infinitely more cumbersome and ineffectual.

The Church is not about policies; it is about a way of life. It is about prayer, liturgy, sharing and social action (Acts 2:42ff; 4:32ff). The real contribution that we make to that life is by living it. If that life is not being lived, there is nothing for the structures and policies to coordinate and encourage.

The richness and initiative of particular groups, parishes, dioceses and regions can show the way to other groups, challenge other groups and give heart to other groups. Living the Christian life is not primarily about changing policies; it is about changing ourselves and changing the world. It is in bringing new life to our communities and our world that we bring new life, and new priorities, programmes and structures, to the Church.

I wonder, in any case, about all this decision making! Where or when does it take place? As I sit through the three days of a Bishops' Meeting I see very few decisions which are made without a great deal of lay input; I see an agenda which is almost entirely set not by the bishops but by all sorts of groups and organisations and individuals who make complaints and suggestions and reports about their activities in the life of the Irish Church; I see scarcely any decisions at all, if by that one means rules or policy options which could in any way restrict the freedom of action of those who seek justice, the building of community and all the other goals put forward by the participants in Teach Bríde.

It is, of course, right that all members of the Church should be heard, for the Holy Spirit is present in all. Those views should be heard first of all in their local communities. It is right that we should work to create many more groups active in prayer, reflection and action for justice. Such groups will influence the Church in many ways through their vitality and their variety. They will influence the Church's life much more profoundly than will the activity of those who give all their attention to policy making. The answers do not lie in the Palace of Oz but in the wisdom, love and courage which the Spirit has already given to his people.

The Christian young people of today have a world to evangelise. The perilous world of the late twentieth century and the twenty-first century needs the Good News and never before have the stakes been so high. Either we find the transforming, hope-giving truth about ourselves and about the God who saves us, and live that truth, or we destroy ourselves. Either we use the marvels of science and technology to make the world more human, more just, more in harmony with the plan of God or we risk using them to make it uninhabitable.

With so much at stake, it is little wonder that people feel impatience and frustration, that they seek answers with increasing desperation. But that, at least, is a sign of hope. There are many people who would never have spent a weekend in Teach Bríde because they feel no anger, only apathy and hopelessness.

With so much at stake, it is vital that the impatience and frustration should not be misdirected, should not be devoted to the search for illusory goals. Powerlessness and despair can be products of the belief that *power is always somewhere else.* Every time one gains access to a new 'source of power' one finds only a Wizard of Oz – no magic, no formula for changing the world, just people like ourselves.

Let us, in God's name, set out on the road of following Christ; let us set out together. The ministers and the structures of the Church exist to help in that task of bringing the Good News to the world. You who are young will have to show us new needs, new challenges, new opportunities, new ways of proclaiming and living the Gospel in the world which is developing. You will have to show us these things not just in words but in action. When we say 'Yes, but . . .' it does not mean that we are being obstructive and negative. It springs from a desire to ensure that your commitment is effective and realistic and that the message which you proclaim and live is the message which we have received.

We are, as Saint Augustine put it, bishops *for* you but Christians *with* you. We are trying, like you, to learn the most effective ways of bringing the faith we have received, the hope which has been given to us and the love to which we are called to the world in which we live. Do not be sidetracked from the way of Christ on to the Yellow Brick Road at the end of which lie only caricatures and disillusionment.

Notes:
1. L, Frank Baum, *The Wizard of Oz*, Puffin Classics 1983, page 135.
2. *Sharing and corresponding in the Church*
   Because the Church is a communion there must be sharing and co-responsibility at all levels. This general principle has to be understood differently in different settings. Since Vatican II, a new type of collaboration between lay people and clergy has happily come about in the Church. The spirit of readiness in which a great number of lay people have offered themselves for the service of the Church, must be counted among the best benefits of the council. In this there is a new experience of the fact that we are all the Church.
   There has often been question in these last years of the vocation and mission of women in the Church. The Church should see that women take their place in the Church in such a way that they can adequately use their proper gifts for the service of the Church, and have a more extensive part in the various fields of the Church's apostolate (cf *Apostolicam Actuositatem* 9). Pastors should

gratefully take up and encourage the collaboration of women in the work of the Church.

The council calls young people the hope of the Church (cf *Gravissimum Educationis* 2). This synod turns to young people with a special love and with great confidence, and looks for much from their generous dedication, urging them to take their place in the mission of the Church and thereby take up and promote dynamically the inheritance of the council.

Because the Church is a communion, the new so-called 'basic communities', if they genuinely live in the unity of the Church, are a true expression of communion and an instrument for fashioning a more profound communion. They thus offer great hope for the life of the Church (cf *Evangelii Nuntiandi* 58).

3. Paul VI, *Evangelii Nuntiandi*, 70.
4. R. Mengus, 'Methode Transcendentale et Revelation, *Nouvelle Revue Theologique,* vol. 102, page 30.